The three witches

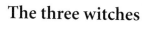

Macduff
(Lord of Fife)

Banquo
(Macbeth's friend)

Ross
(a Scottish noble)

The Shakespeare Collection

MACBETH

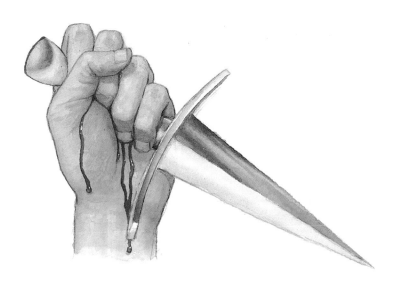

RETOLD BY ANTHONY MASTERS

Illustrated by Stephen Player

HODDER
Wayland

 *Character list:*

Macbeth

Lady Macbeth

Duncan
(King of Scotland)

Donalbain
(Duncan's son)

Malcolm
(Duncan's son)

"*I*'ve never seen anything like it!"

Macbeth and his great friend, Banquo, stared at the three witches in horrified amazement. With their withered skins, their wild and straggling hair and their bearded chins, they were a fearful sight.

Macbeth and Banquo, two Scottish generals, were returning home after defeating the invading Norwegians. Their path led across a wind-blasted heath where the three witches often met.

"We can't avoid them," Macbeth told Banquo. "Let's see what they want... Good evening," Macbeth began politely. But each witch put a skinny, stick-like finger to her lips, asking for silence. "What do you want?" he demanded.

The first witch grinned at Macbeth. "Good evening, Lord of Glamis."

He shrugged. "That's the title I'm known by. What do you want?" he repeated.

The second witch grinned even more widely, showing the black stumps of her teeth. "Greetings, Lord of Cawdor."

"I don't have any claim to *that* title." Macbeth was becoming uneasy.

The third witch smiled a cat-like smile. "Welcome, Macbeth, King of Scotland."

Macbeth could never be King of Scotland. His cousin, Duncan, was already king and he had sons who would reign when he died. But Macbeth knew that witches were able to see into the future. Could this be *his* future?

Then one of the witches turned to Banquo and told him a riddle. "You'll be a lesser man than Macbeth. But you'll also be a greater one. Not so happy, but much happier." Banquo would never be King of Scotland, she added, but his sons would be kings instead.

When Macbeth and Banquo tried to ask more questions, the three old hags vanished. The heath was left deserted, with just a whisper of a foul-smelling breeze.

Suddenly two horsemen came thundering across the heath. As the horses sweated to a halt, the two Scottish noblemen, Ross and Angus, jumped down from their saddles.

"We've been sent by the king." Ross was breathless. "He has heard how you defeated the traitor Lord Cawdor after he'd joined the enemy. He has stripped him of his title and is giving it to you, Macbeth. A great honour."

It certainly was. Macbeth was so taken aback that he didn't know what to say. Part of the witches' prophecy had just come true. But what about the rest of it? Could he really be crowned King of Scotland one day? A tiny seed of ambition began to grow inside him.

$\mathcal{M}$acbeth sent a letter to his wife, telling her all
that had happened. Lady Macbeth had always
been an ambitious woman and when Macbeth
arrived home, she suggested a daring plan. They
should make the witches' prophecy come true –
by murdering the king. King Duncan and his
two sons, Donalbain and Malcolm, were all too
conveniently visiting the castle that evening.

"It's the chance of a lifetime," insisted Lady
Macbeth.

Glamis was a beautiful castle. Swallows had built nests under the buttresses and there was an atmosphere of peace, love and comfort which immediately made King Duncan feel welcome. Tired after his journey, he went to bed early while two of his grooms slept in his state room to guard him.

$\mathcal{M}$acbeth was terrified by the decision that he and Lady Macbeth had made. How could he murder his guest, his king?

He summoned a servant and sent Lady Macbeth an urgent message. "Tell your mistress to ring the bell when my drink is ready," he said. He knew that Lady Macbeth would realize what he really meant: "Ring the bell when it is safe for me to kill the king."

Macbeth then had nothing to do but wait.

Standing alone, time seemed to go so slowly, waiting for the sound of the bell. Staring into the shadows, Macbeth was horrified to see a dagger floating in the air, just in front of him.

"Is this really a dagger I can see before me?" he whispered, trying to grab it. The dagger's handle was pointing towards him but he was clutching at nothing.

Macbeth tried to convince himself that the dagger was just the creation of his guilty mind, but it continued to hover in front of him.

Suddenly its clean blade became stained with blood and Macbeth looked nervously over his shoulder.

"It must be witchcraft," he muttered, sure that his terrible plan had been betrayed. "I beg the very earth itself not to listen to my footsteps," he pleaded. "Don't let the stones cry out and give me away."

Then Macbeth heard the signal. The bell was ringing. It already sounded like King Duncan's death knell.

As Macbeth silently entered the king's
bedchamber, Lady Macbeth reached the room
next door. Now it was her turn to wait.

"He must be doing it now. I've drugged
the grooms' drinks," she muttered, trying to
reassure herself. "I've done everything I can."

18

Then she heard a voice from the king's bedchamber asking, "Who's there?"

Immediately Lady Macbeth was terrified that one of the grooms had woken before her husband had been able to kill the king.

"I laid the daggers ready," she whispered. "He couldn't miss them. If the king hadn't looked so much like my father as he slept I could have killed him myself."

But Macbeth had not failed her.

"I've done it," he said as he joined his wife, and she felt a wave of relief. "It was terrible," Macbeth told her. "One of the grooms cried out: 'Glamis has murdered sleep and therefore Cawdor shall sleep no more. Macbeth shall sleep no more.' "

Lady Macbeth wouldn't allow him to continue. "You had to do it," she insisted. "Soon we'll be King and Queen of Scotland. But why didn't you leave the daggers in the king's chamber? You'll have to take them back."

Macbeth would not go back to the bloody room. So Lady Macbeth sent him to wash Duncan's blood from his hands. Then she took the daggers, moving cautiously through the candle-lit corridors once more.

When she reached the king's bedchamber, Lady Macbeth hurriedly wiped his blood from the blades of the daggers on to the cheeks of the drunken, still sleeping grooms. Now it would look as if *they* were the murderers.

In the morning, Duncan's dead body was discovered.

"This is dreadful!" said Macbeth, openly weeping. "The King's been murdered."

"How dreadful that such a thing should happen in our house," cried Lady Macbeth.

To cover his tracks, Macbeth killed Duncan's two guards – supposedly in fury at their terrible crime. The whole court was in a frenzy of shock.

Realizing that their lives might be in danger, too, Duncan's sons knew that they had to escape.

"I'll go to England," Malcolm told Donalbain. "You travel to Ireland. I fear that none of us are safe here."

$\mathcal{A}$s the witches had promised, Macbeth was soon crowned King of Scotland.

But the witches had also said that Macbeth's children would not inherit the throne. Instead, Banquo's son would be crowned king and Banquo's descendants would rule Scotland.

Macbeth was not prepared to accept this. Now he had tasted power, he was determined to hang on to it. He began to plot against Banquo.

$\mathcal{A}$ great banquet was organized at Macbeth's castle and all the nobility were invited to stay, including Banquo and his son, Fleance.

"I think we'll go out riding this afternoon," Banquo told Macbeth. "But we'll be back in time for the feast."

Macbeth smiled. This gave him just the opportunity he wanted.

As Banquo and Fleance rode back to the castle through the woods in the moonlight, Banquo was uneasy. He kept thinking about the witches' prophecy, some of which had already come true. He and Fleance had heard rumours that Macbeth was involved in Duncan's murder.

Banquo reined in his horse. "What's that?" he whispered.

"Nothing, father," replied Fleance. "Just an animal rustling in the bushes."

Suddenly a group of men broke cover.

Although they both put up a fight, in the end Banquo was stabbed to death. Horrified at his father's brutal murder, Fleance made his escape.

Meanwhile, just before the banquet started, Macbeth turned to one of his courtiers and asked, "Where have Banquo and Fleance got to? It's not like them to be late for the feast." But he had already heard the news that Banquo was dead – and that Fleance had escaped.

And as he spoke, Banquo's ghost walked slowly towards him, placing itself on the very chair that he was about to sit on. Macbeth froze, unable to move, staring at his dead friend, appalled at what he had done.

But everyone else only saw Macbeth staring at an empty chair and thought that he had been taken ill.

"What are you doing?" hissed the queen, but Macbeth didn't reply. He was shaking with fear and likely to give them both away.

The queen hurriedly dismissed her guests, making the excuse that her husband was sick.

"You must pull yourself together," she urged Macbeth later.

But Macbeth grew more and more unnerved. He was unable to sleep. He was sure that Banquo's ghost had come for revenge. Fleance's escape also worried him. What's more, an important Scottish noble, Macduff, had failed to attend the banquet. There was a rumour that he had gone to England to raise an army to invade Scotland.

Macbeth decided to visit the witches again.
After all, it was their fault for putting temptation
in his way. Now he wanted to know what his
chances were of surviving as King.

*T*he witches were huddled in a cave near
the windswept heath. They were preparing
a disgusting brew in their magic cauldron
to conjure up spirits to foretell the future.

"You must tell me more of the prophecy,"
urged Macbeth.

But the witches wouldn't listen, they only
stirred their cauldron and chanted:

"Double, double, toil and trouble,
Fire, burn; and cauldron bubble.
Fillet of a fenny snake,
In the cauldron, boil and bake;
Eye of newt, and toe of frog,
Wool of bat—"

"You must answer me!" cried Macbeth in frustration. "Let me see the future."

Without another word the witches called up the spirits. The first was a warrior's head and had a warning for Macbeth: "Beware of the Lord of Fife. Beware Macduff..."

Macbeth nodded. He was already suspicious of Macduff for not attending his banquet. Now he knew that Macduff could not be trusted.

The second spirit rose up in the form of a
bloodied child and told Macbeth to be bold and
determined as 'no man born of woman' would
harm him. Again he felt reassured.

Finally, the third spirit appeared, this time
in the shape of a crowned child with a tree in
his hand.

The child said, "You'll never be defeated until
Birnam Wood starts moving towards Dunsinane
Hill."

Macbeth laughed in relief, knowing that
a forest couldn't possibly move. "But tell me
something else," he asked. "Will Banquo's son
ever become King of Scotland?"

As he spoke, the witches' cauldron sank into the ground and Macbeth heard the sound of strange, haunting music. Then, eight shadowy kings rose up, the last holding a glass which showed a procession of many more ghost-like kings. The ghost of Banquo, covered in blood, stood pointing at them.

With a sinking heart Macbeth realized that all these kings were Banquo's descendants. Whatever was going to happen next?

Only the witches could tell him, but when Macbeth turned to ask them he found that they had vanished.

When Macbeth got back to the castle, one of the nobles brought the news that Macduff had sailed for England. "He's going to join Malcolm's army. They're going to invade Scotland and put Malcolm on the throne."

Calmly and coldly, Macbeth took his terrible revenge. He sent armed men to Macduff's castle, with orders to kill Lady Macduff, her children and even her servants.

The other Scottish lords, horrified at the bloodthirsty murders, immediately joined Malcolm and Macduff's invading army.

Meanwhile, the queen became ill. While Macbeth had become more ruthless, she had become weaker, racked with fear and guilt. She had taken to sleepwalking, roaming the castle at night, convinced she couldn't wash the blood of the murders off her hands. The doctors could do nothing for her.

Macbeth was preparing for Malcolm's invasion when a servant came running to his room.

"The queen, my lord, is dead," he stammered, and Macbeth shivered, knowing he was now alone.

Now Macbeth could only wish for his own death. All too well aware of the approaching army, he decided to shut himself up in his castle.

Almost immediately, however, another messenger, pale and shaking, was shown in to see Macbeth.

"What is it?" demanded the king.

"I was standing guard on the hill when I saw – when I saw – the woods at Birnam begin to move."

Macbeth remembered the witches' prophecy. They had told him that nothing could harm him until Birnam Wood came to Dunsinane Hill. And now the wood was moving!

*I*n truth the wood hadn't moved at all. Malcolm was a skilful general and had told his soldiers to cut down branches of the trees and use them as camouflage as they moved towards the castle.

Yet, still refusing to admit his brief reign as King of Scotland was over, Macbeth took all he had left of his followers and attacked Malcolm's much larger army.

"We'll destroy them," he said. "We've *got* to destroy them."

Macbeth and Macduff came face to face and fought viciously. "You killed my wife and children," Macduff yelled at Macbeth. "You're a tyrant and a murderer."

But Macbeth remembered the words of the spirit that the three witches had summoned up and clung to his one last hope.

"You can't kill me," Macbeth told Macduff. "No one who was born of a woman can hurt me."

But Macduff only smiled triumphantly. "Didn't you know, Macbeth?" he said. "I was taken from my mother's womb before I was due to be born. So I wasn't born naturally at all."

At this, Macbeth felt a surge of panic, but he made one last desperate effort. He threw himself at Macduff and they fought even more viciously than before.

Then Macduff drew on his last ounce of strength, swung his sword and Macbeth's head rolled on to the ground, coming to rest at his feet.

Macduff bent down and picked up the severed head and made a present of it to the lawful king, Malcolm.

With Macbeth dead, the nobles all hailed Malcolm as their rightful king. A new time of peace was dawning in Scotland.

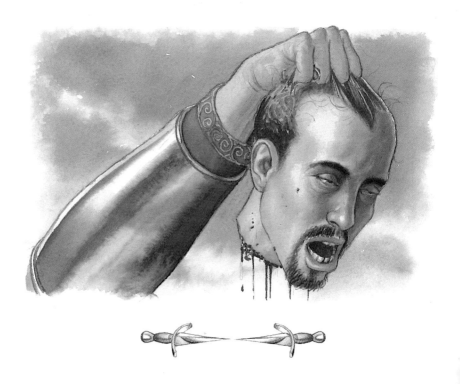